A Very Mice Color ~y book!

Volume 2

House-Mouse Designs®

Amanda   Monica   Mudpie   Maxwell   Muzzy

Frolicsome Fall with the House-Mouse® Family

Meet Our Artist, Ellen Jareckie:

Ellen was born in Bennington, Vermont in 1959. As a child, she spent much of her spare time drawing. She also kept a variety of pets throughout her childhood, which included a pig named Pipsqueak (who was raised on a bottle) a quail, some lizards and, of course, mice. When Ellen was introduced to her first mouse, it was love at first sight, and the beginning of a lifelong interest, which would eventually lead to the creation of House-Mouse Designs®. Ellen began House-Mouse® in 1980 with business partner, Barry Percy. It started out as a relatively small mail-order/greeting card business selling Ellen's artwork on cards, calendars and paper items featuring a delightful line of mice, as featured in this coloring book. Ellen uses pencil and ink and watercolor to create all of her images out of her studio in Shelburne, Vermont. She depicts her characters in a life-size, human environment, which is designed to give the viewer a "mouse's-eye" view of the world. In addition to the mice Ellen has also created several other animal characters -- her bunnies line is called HappyHoppers® and a line of bears, is her Gruffies® brand and a host of others in her House-Mouse Friends® line featuring cats and the Wee Poppets® hamsters. In addition to drawing exclusively for House-Mouse Designs®, Ellen has volunteered for many years to help rehabilitate injured and orphaned wildlife, some of which have been the inspiration behind her images and can be seen interacting with the mice, in her artwork. She currently volunteers for the American Red Cross association, as well.

Meet our Mice Characters:

See color images of all five House-Mouse Designs® characters on the back cover of this coloring book.

Amanda: Amanda has fawn colored fur and her ears are a bit large. She is the caretaker of the House-Mouse® gang. Amanda tends to be a bit bossy, though truth be known, the others love that she takes charge.

Maxwell: Maxwell is reddish-brown in color and he has a perpetually curled tail. He is rather mischievous and he spends most of his time pulling pranks on the other mice. Maxwell loves to create a bit of chaos, but it's all in good cheer and good fun.

Mudpie: Mudpie has brown fur and a nick in his left ear. His two favorite activities are eating and sleeping. He's a true mouse-potato. He could use a little exercise but isn't likely to begin a fitness routine anytime soon. Mudpie takes each day as it comes and hopes you'll do the same!

Monica: Monica is gray with a tiny body and big feet. She is very innocent and sweet. She is the baby of the group, which makes her a little bit spoiled. Spoiled with love and tenderness, but spoiled, nonetheless.

Muzzy: Muzzy is fuzzy and his fur is a bit long and mushroom gray in color. He is the most curious of the five House-Mouse® mice. Needless to say, his favorite way to pass the time is to investigate ... anything and everything. Perhaps you can help Muzzy find out where these mouse-prints lead.

For more information on our wacky, whimsical line of House-Mouse® mice, please go to our website at
www.house-mouse.com

Leafy sleep!

Monica

Sunny seat!

Mudpie

Junior juggler!

Maxwell & Monica

Crazy for candy corn!

Mudpie & Monica

Fall time fun!

Amanda, Mudpie, Monica & Muzzy

Happy harvesters!

Muzzy, Amanda, Mudpie, Friends & Maxwell

Leap of faith!

Amanda, Maxwell, Monica & Mudpie

Cuppa comfort!

Maxwell & Mudpie

Nutty & nice!

Amanda, Maxwell, Mudpie, Monica & Friend

Fall time flyers!

Amanda, Monica, Muzzy & Mudpie

cozy costumes!

Mudpie, Maxwell, Monica & Amanda

school yard scramble!

Amanda, Monica, Muzzy, Maxwell & Mudpie

Haunted bird house!

Monica, Mudpie & Friends

school supplies!

Maxwell, Muzzy & Mudpie

Cocoa-casion!

Amanda, Mudpie, Monica, Muzzy & Maxwell

rainy day roost!

Muzzy, Amanda, Mudpie, Monica & Friend

Wool for warmth!

Maxwell & Amanda

Feasting family and friends!

Maxwell, Friends, Mudpie, Amanda, Monica & Muzzy

Leafy launch!

Mudpie & Monica

Mice costumes!

Mudpie, Monica & Maxwell

Thankful for treats!

Monica, Muzzy & Mudpie